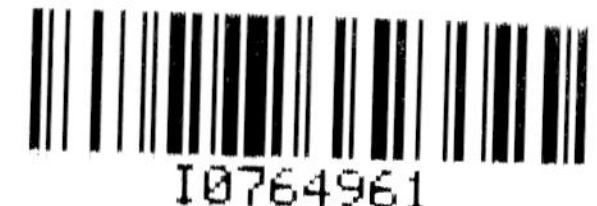

Beautiful Winter

An Adult Coloring book

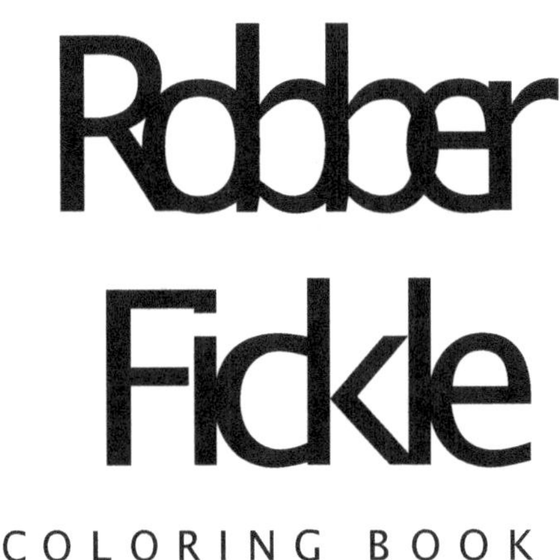

For Any Question and Suggestions
robberfickle@gmail.com

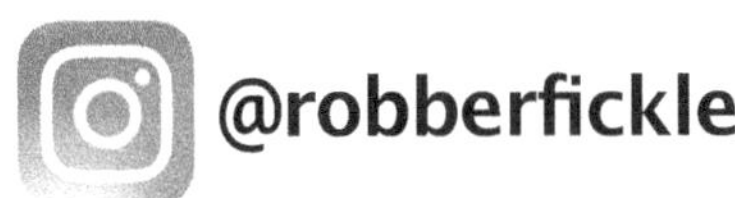 **@robberfickle**

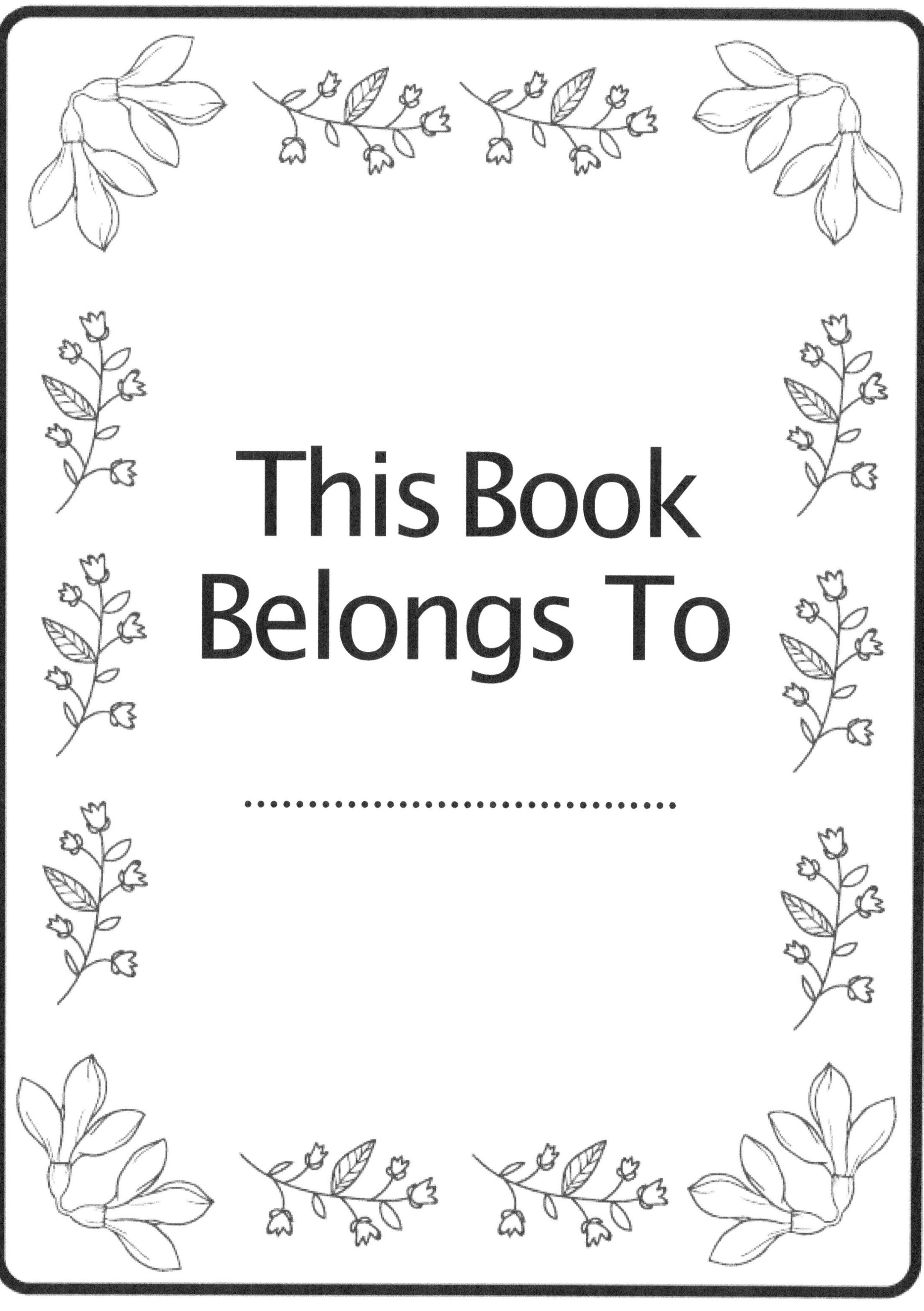

This Book Belongs To

....

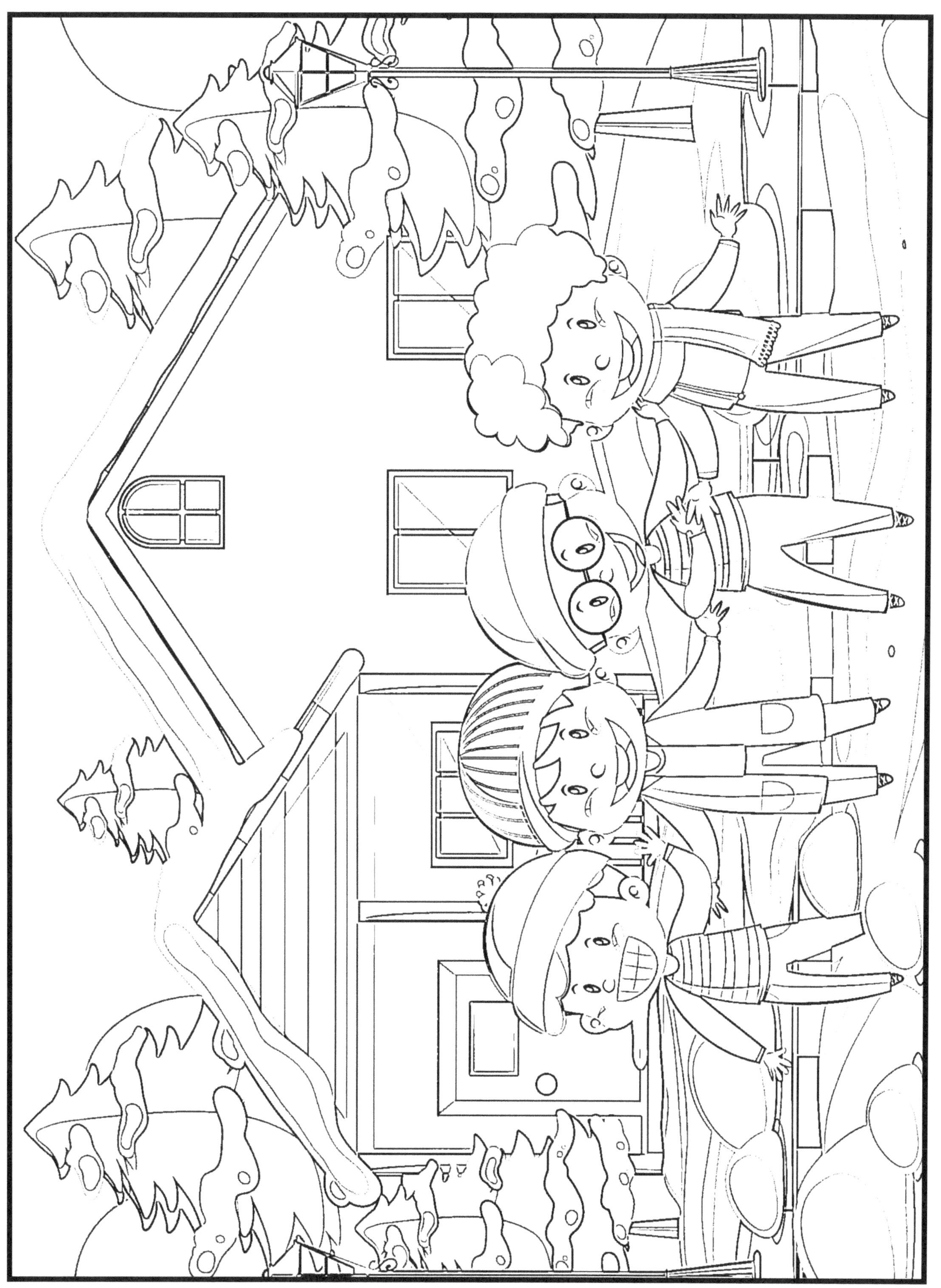

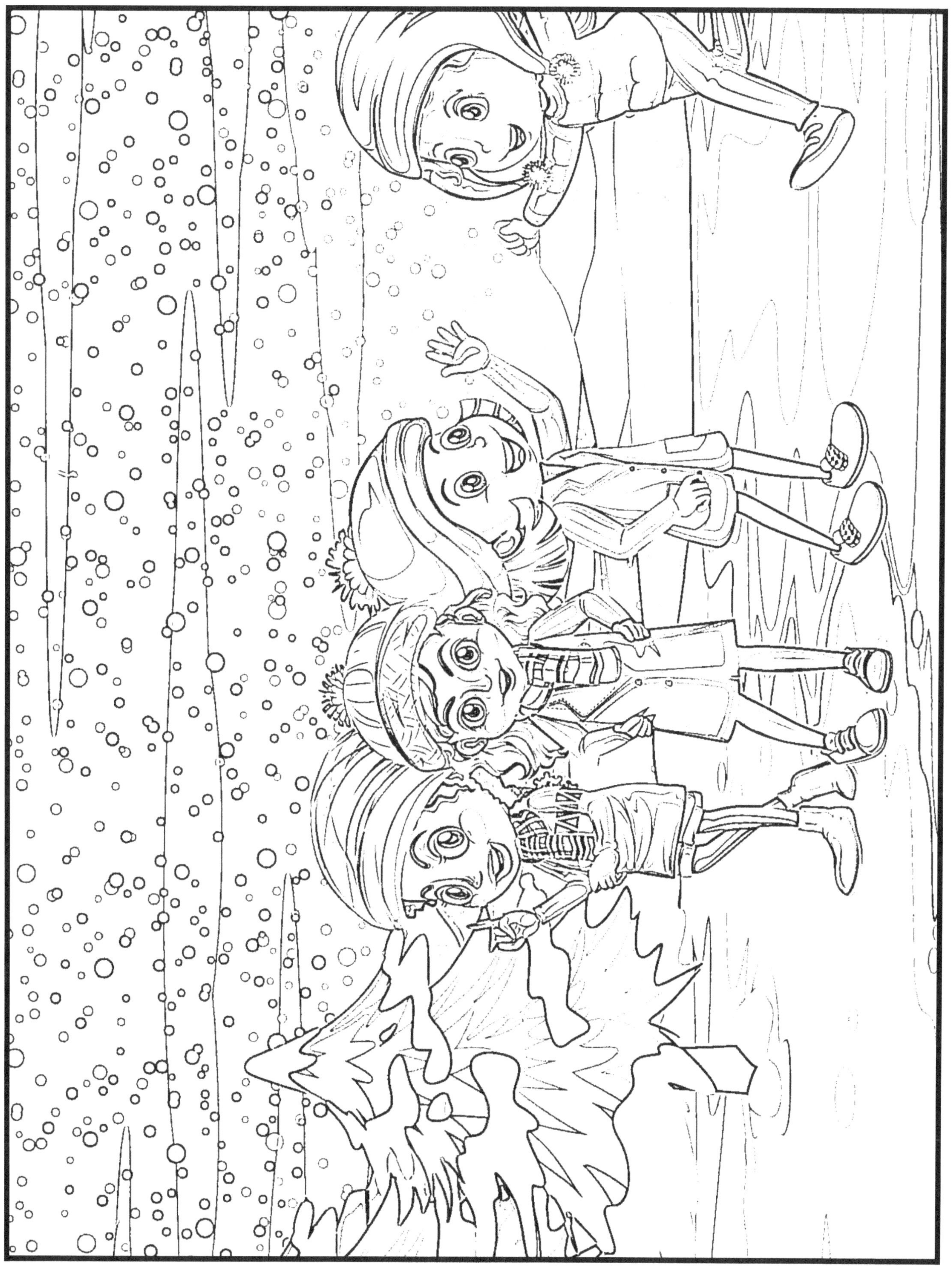

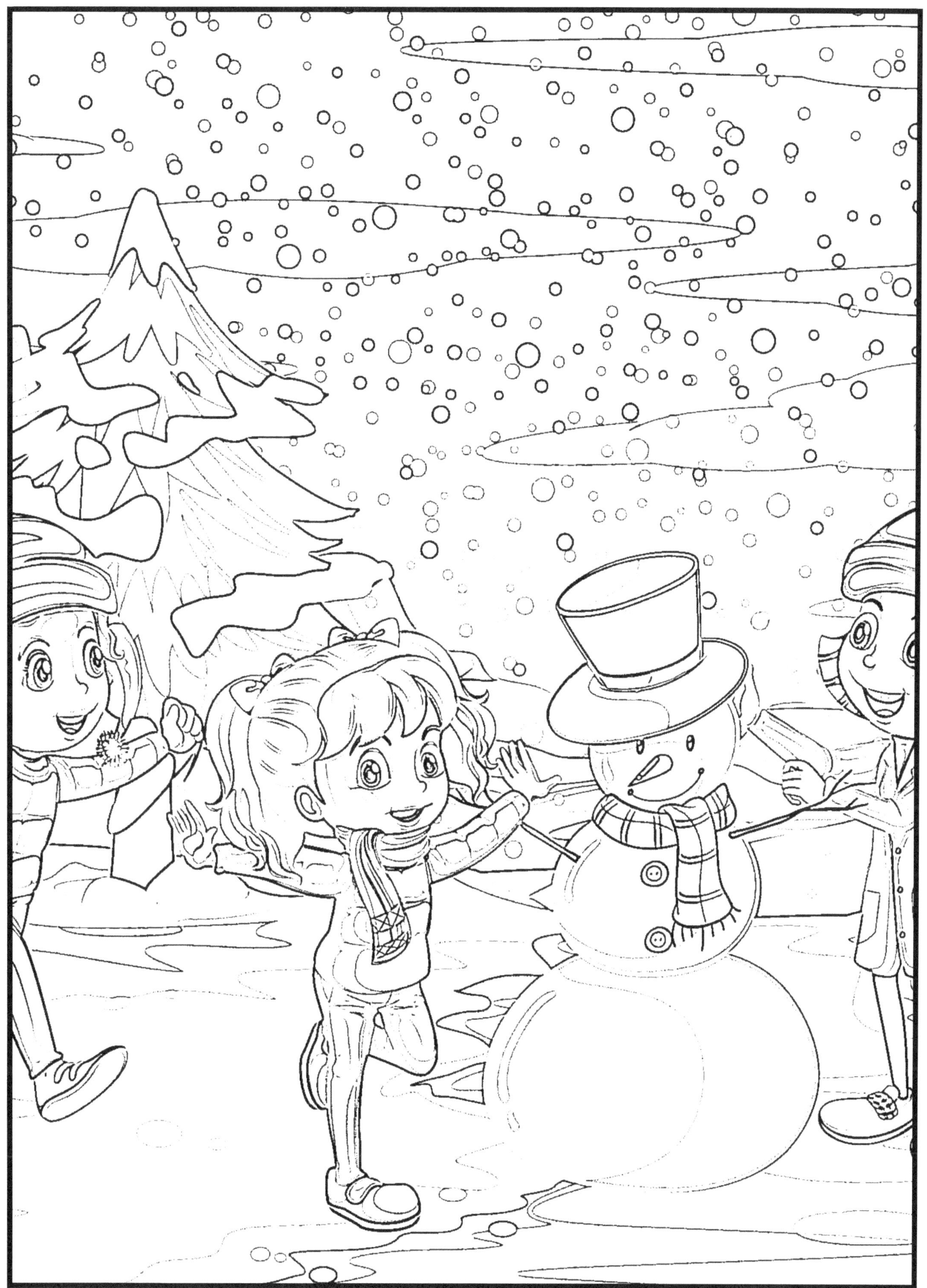

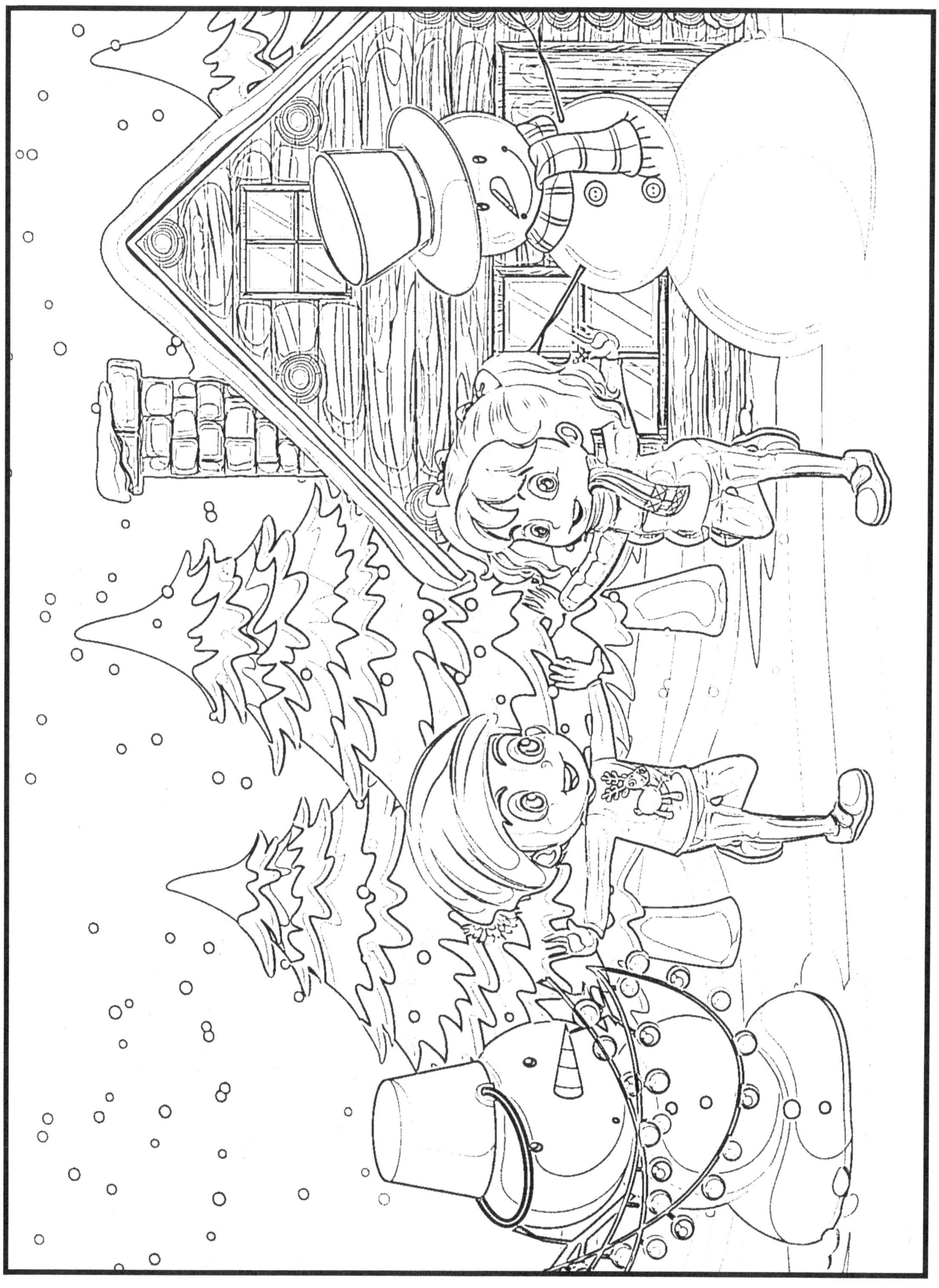

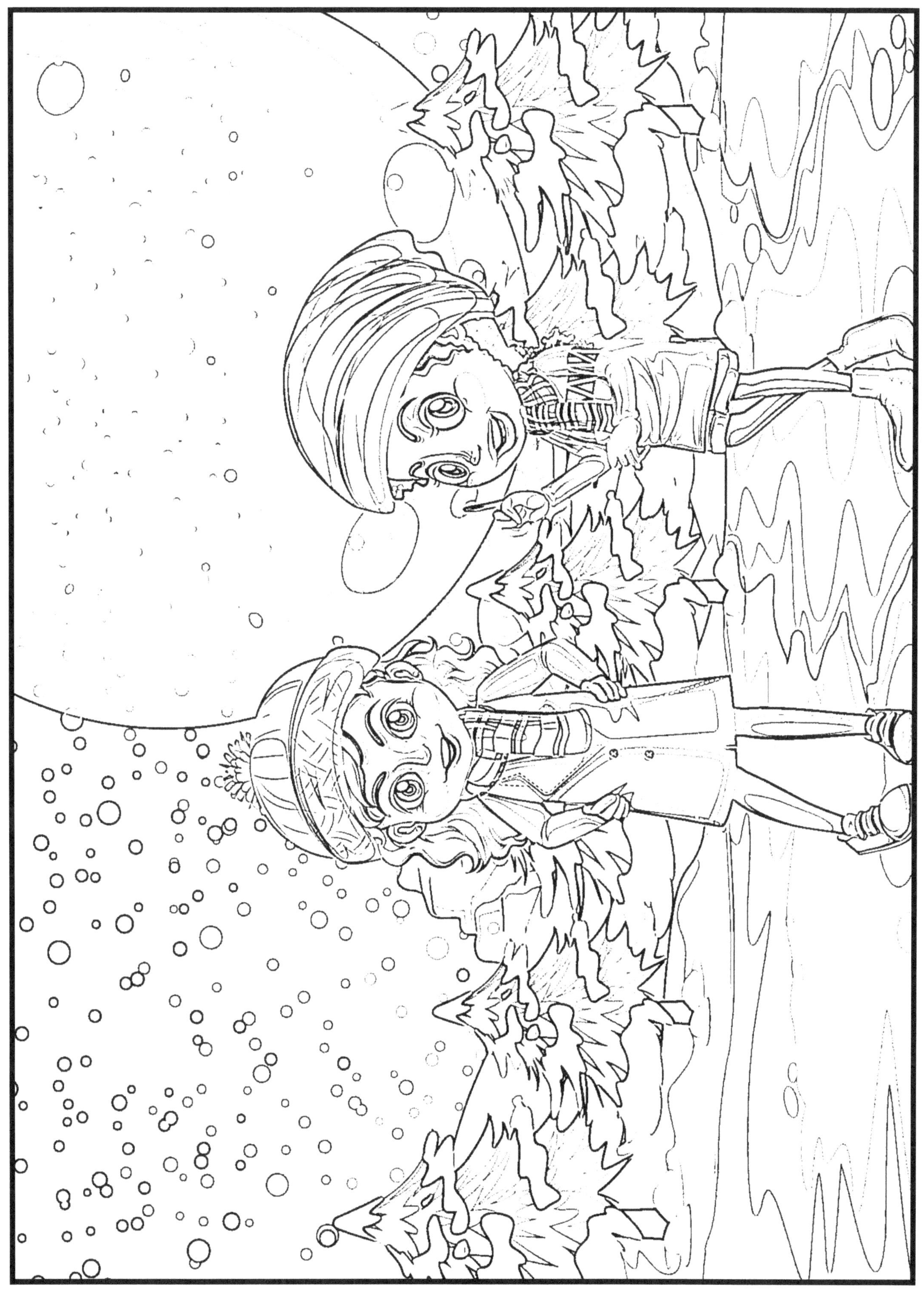

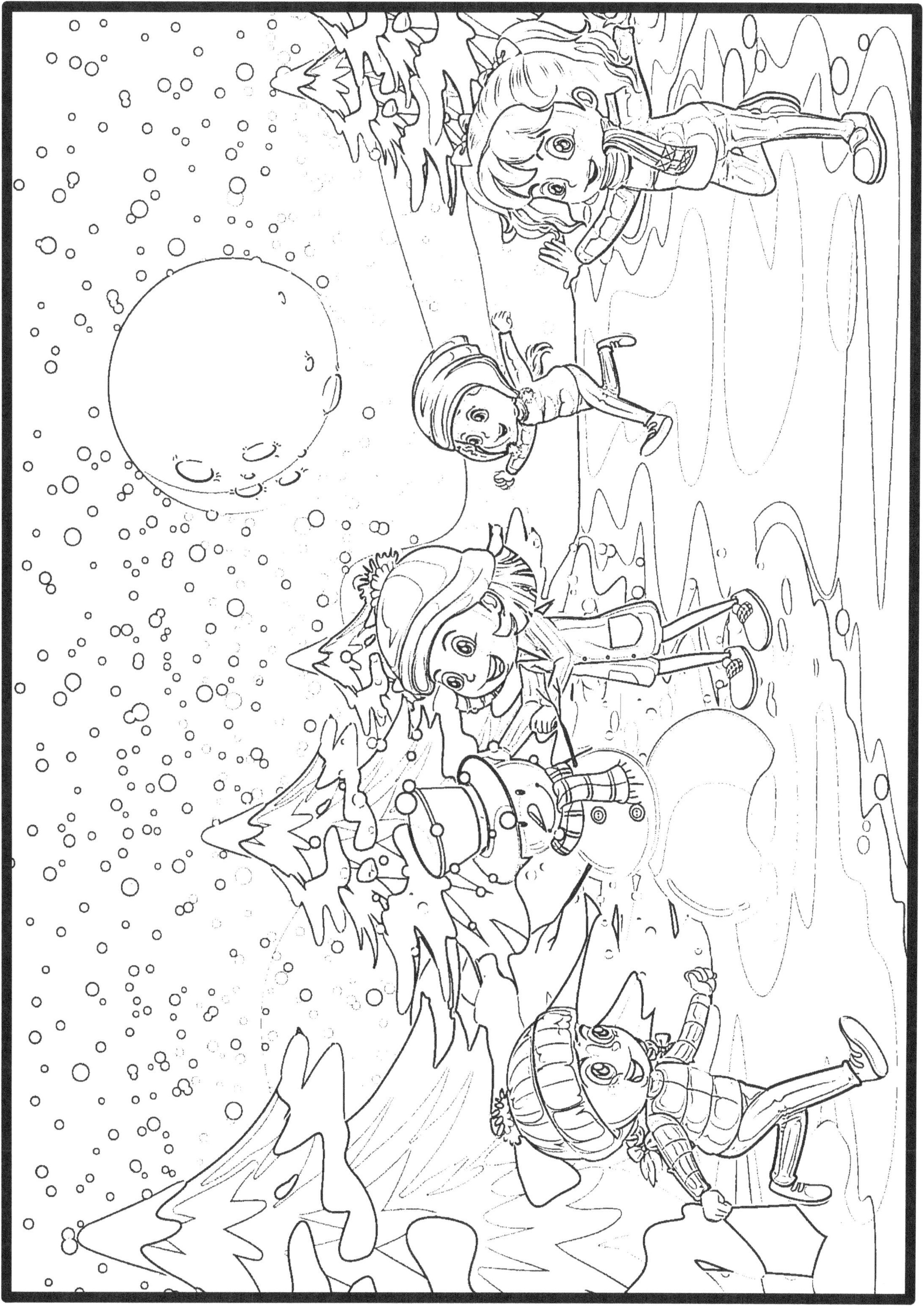

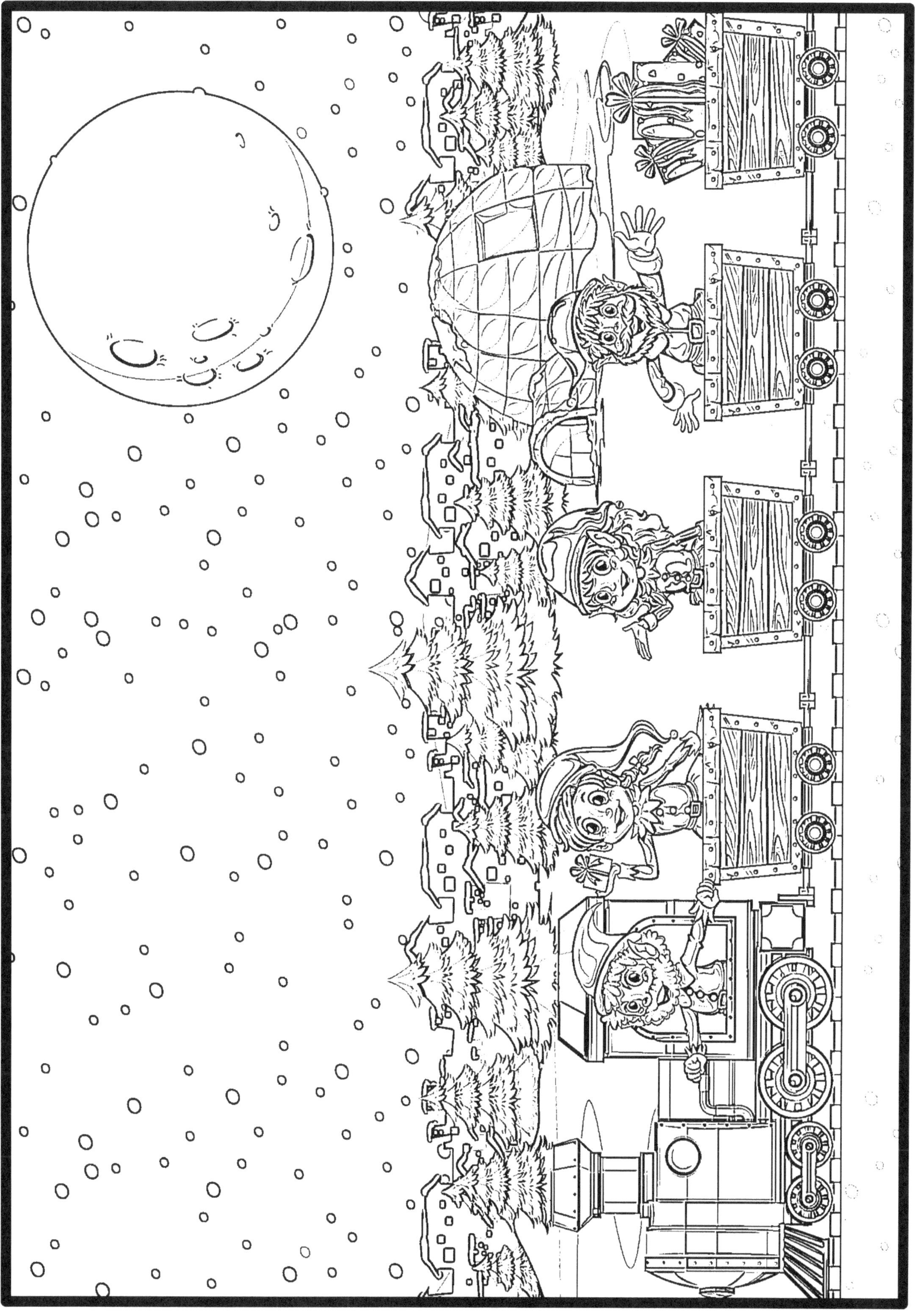

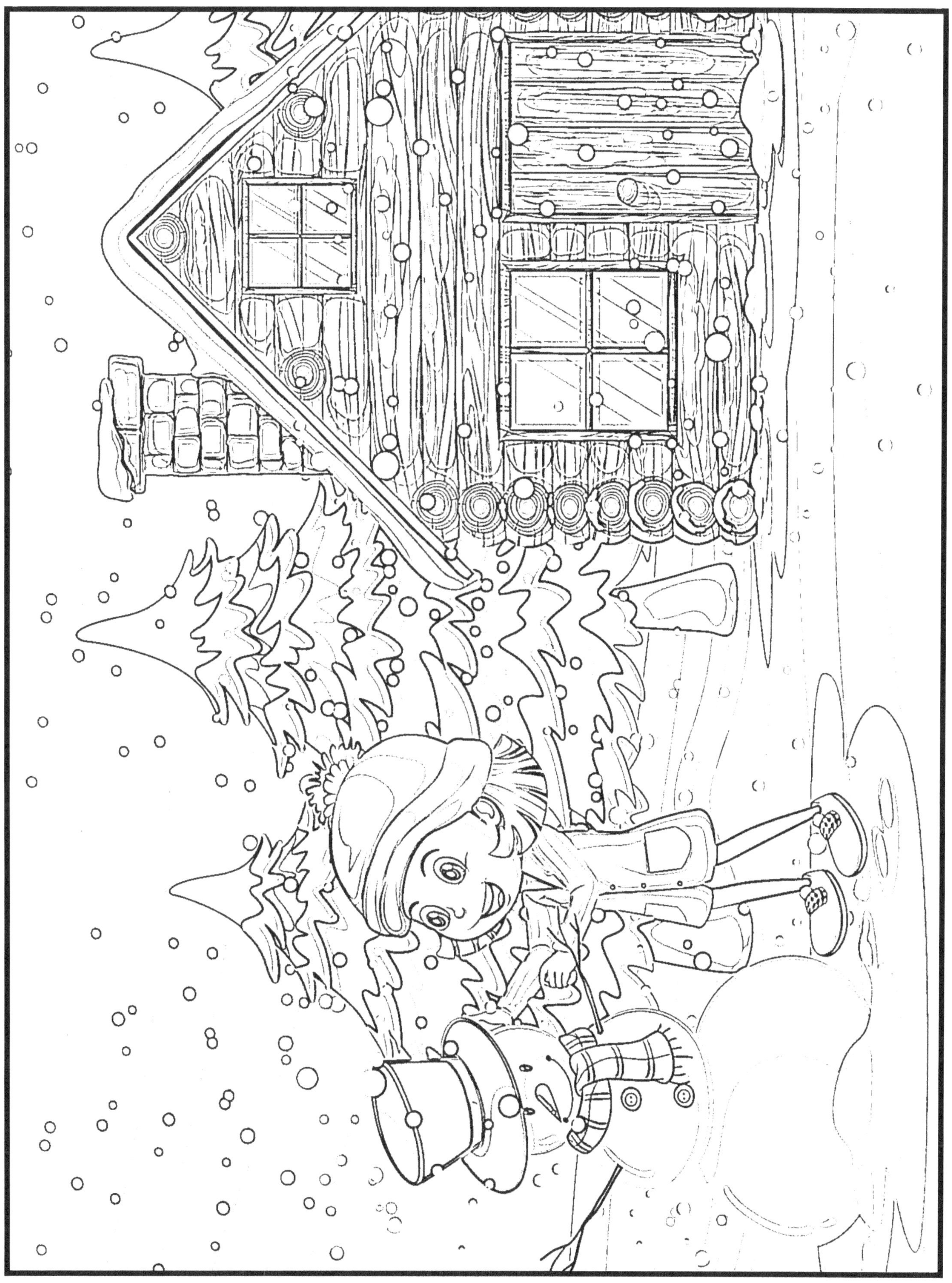

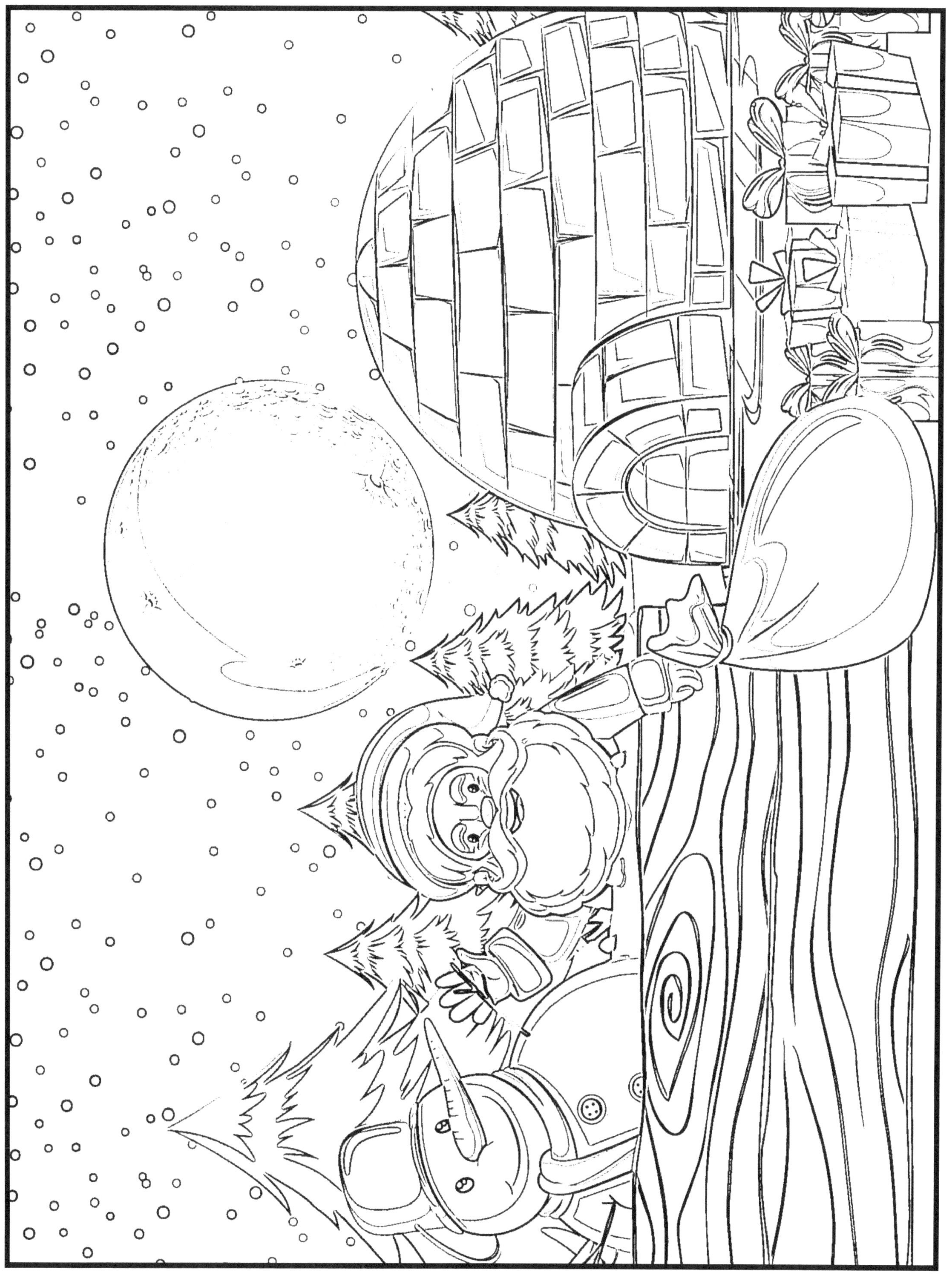

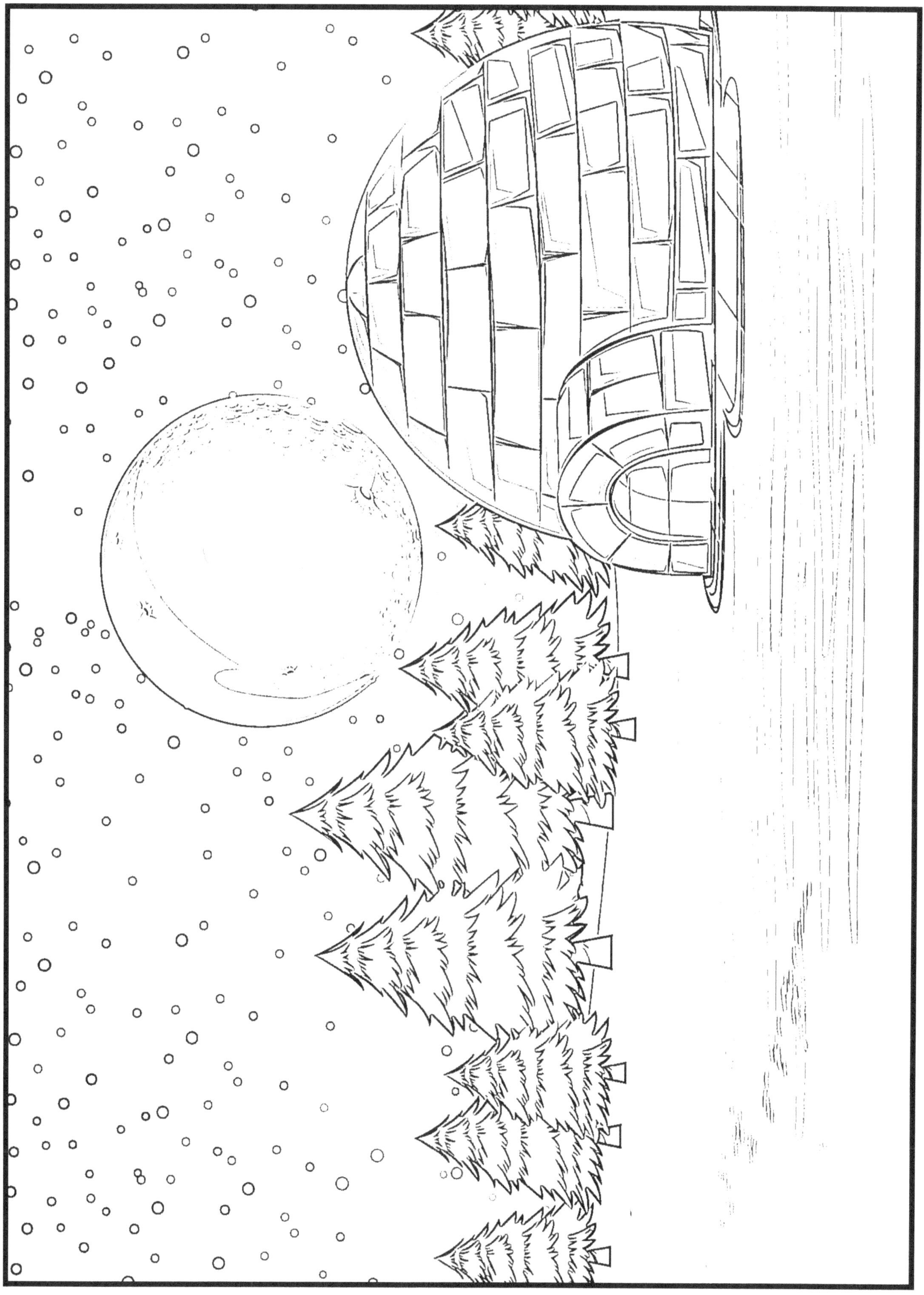

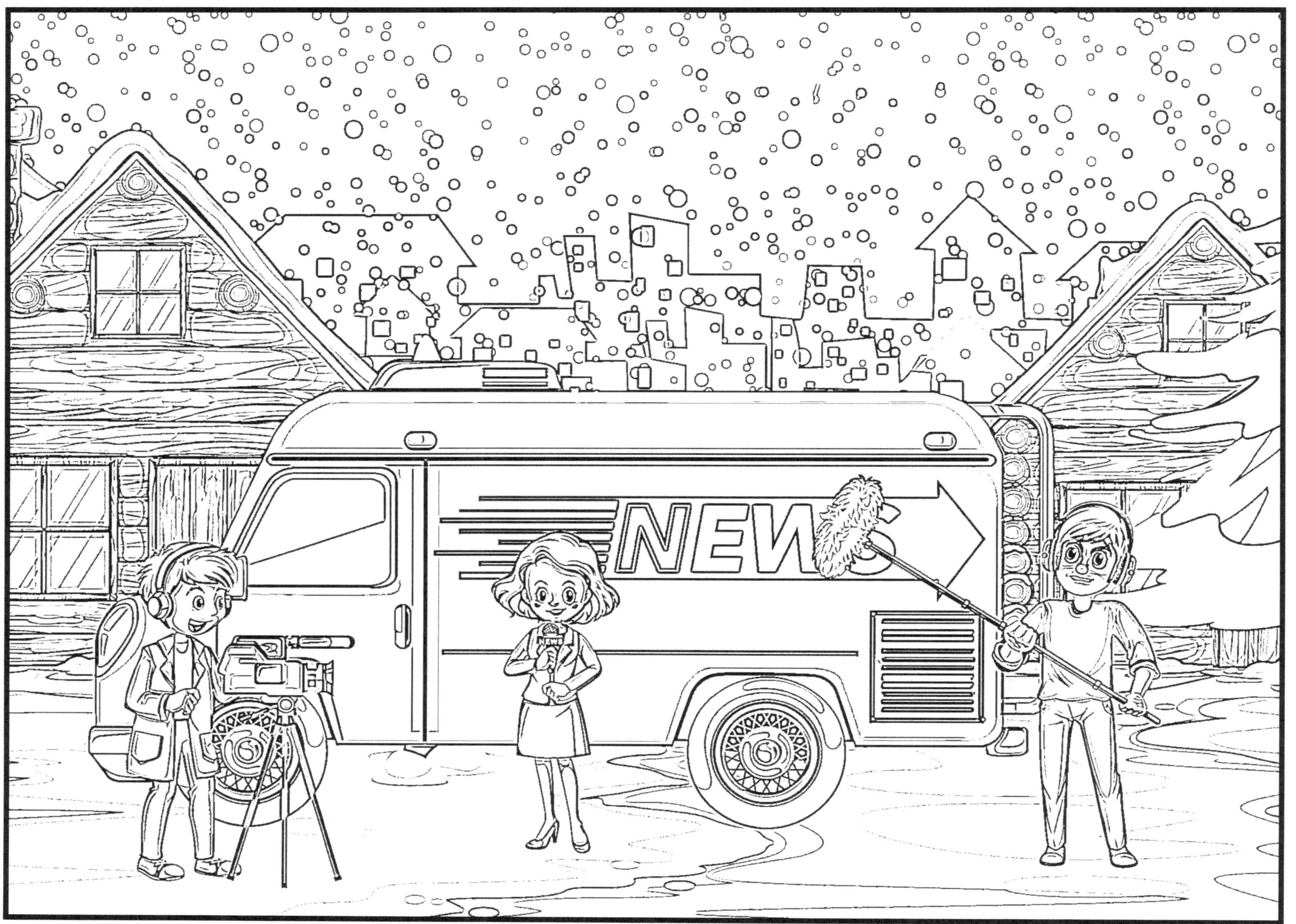
NEWS

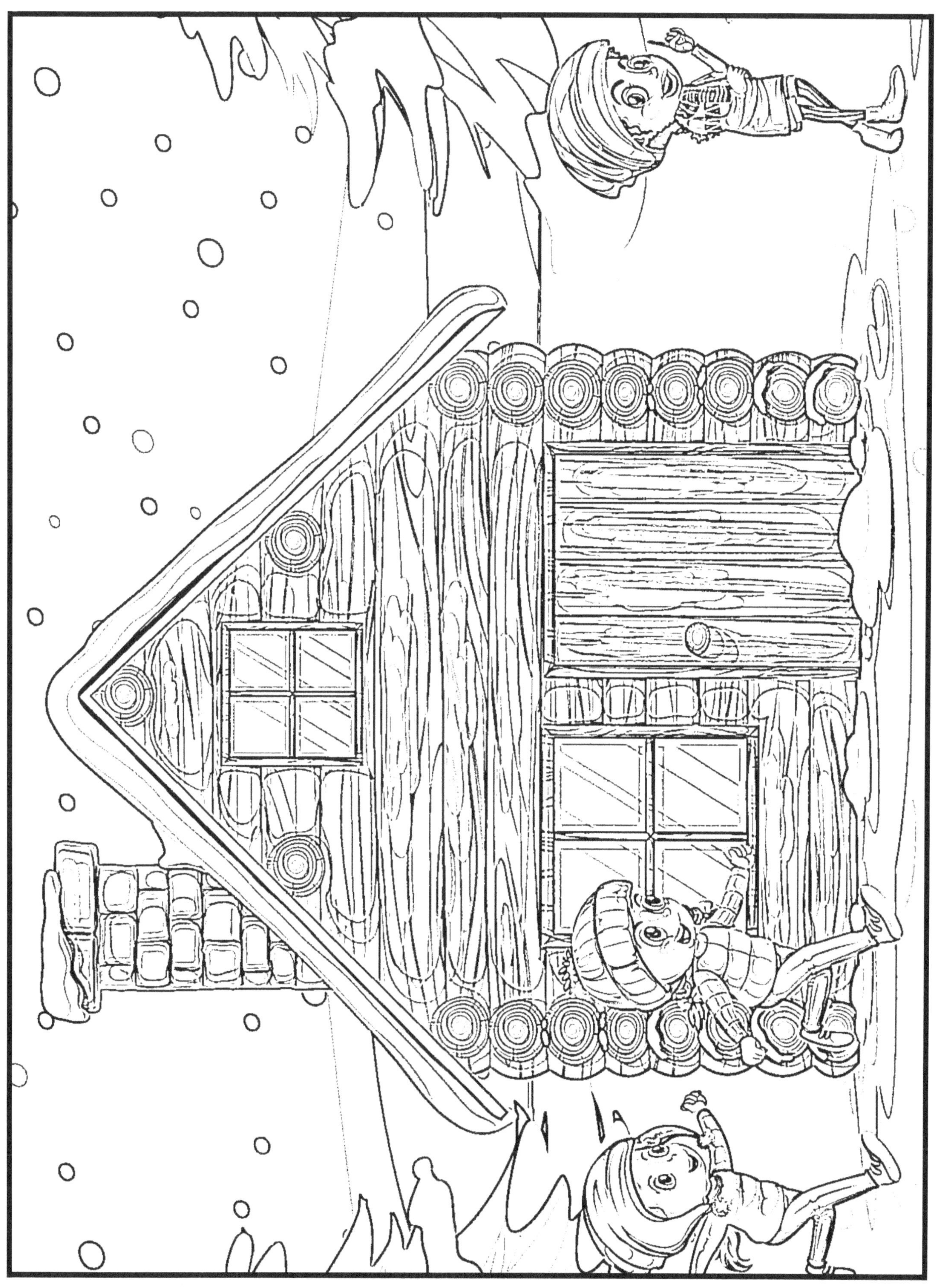

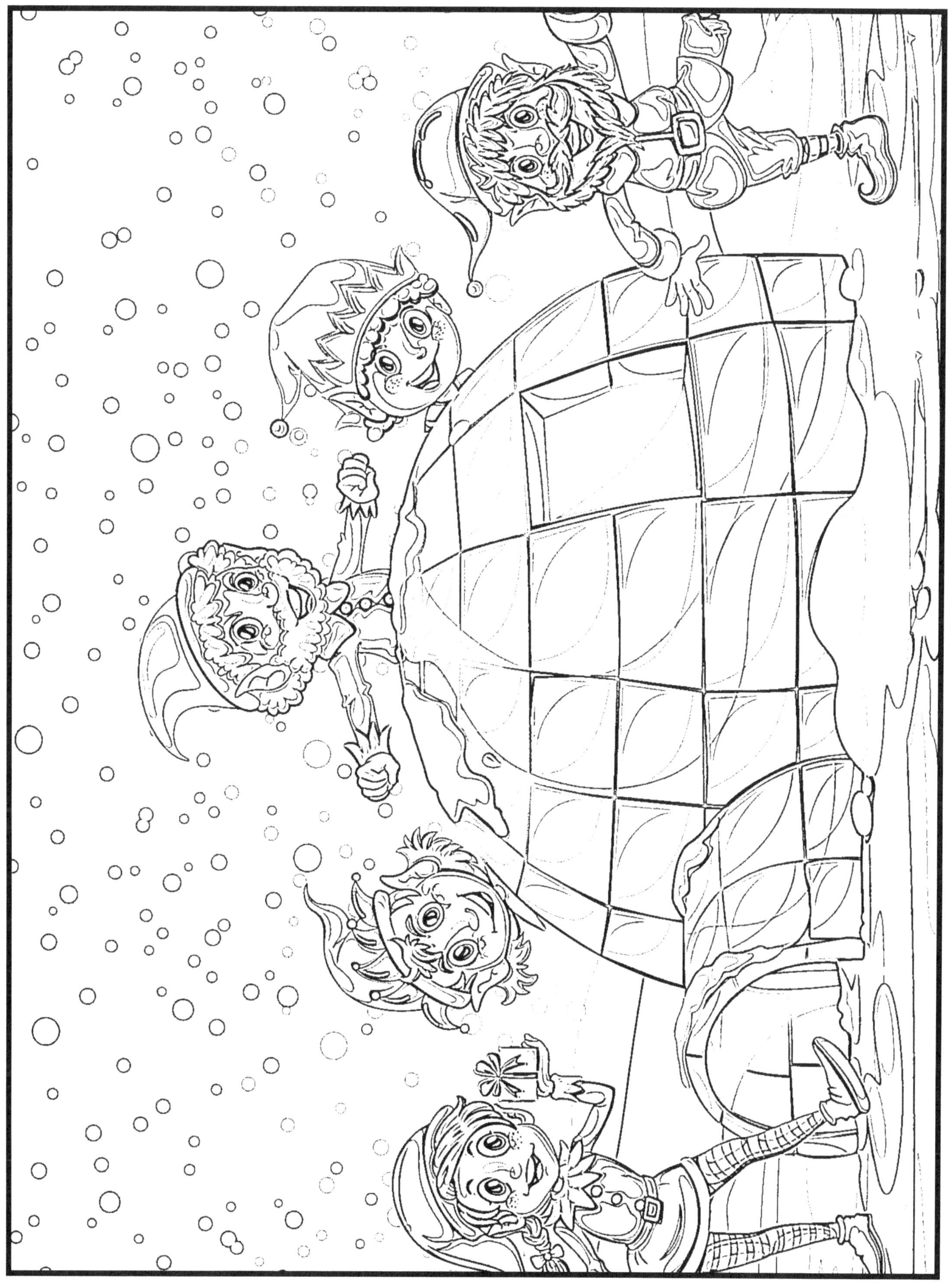

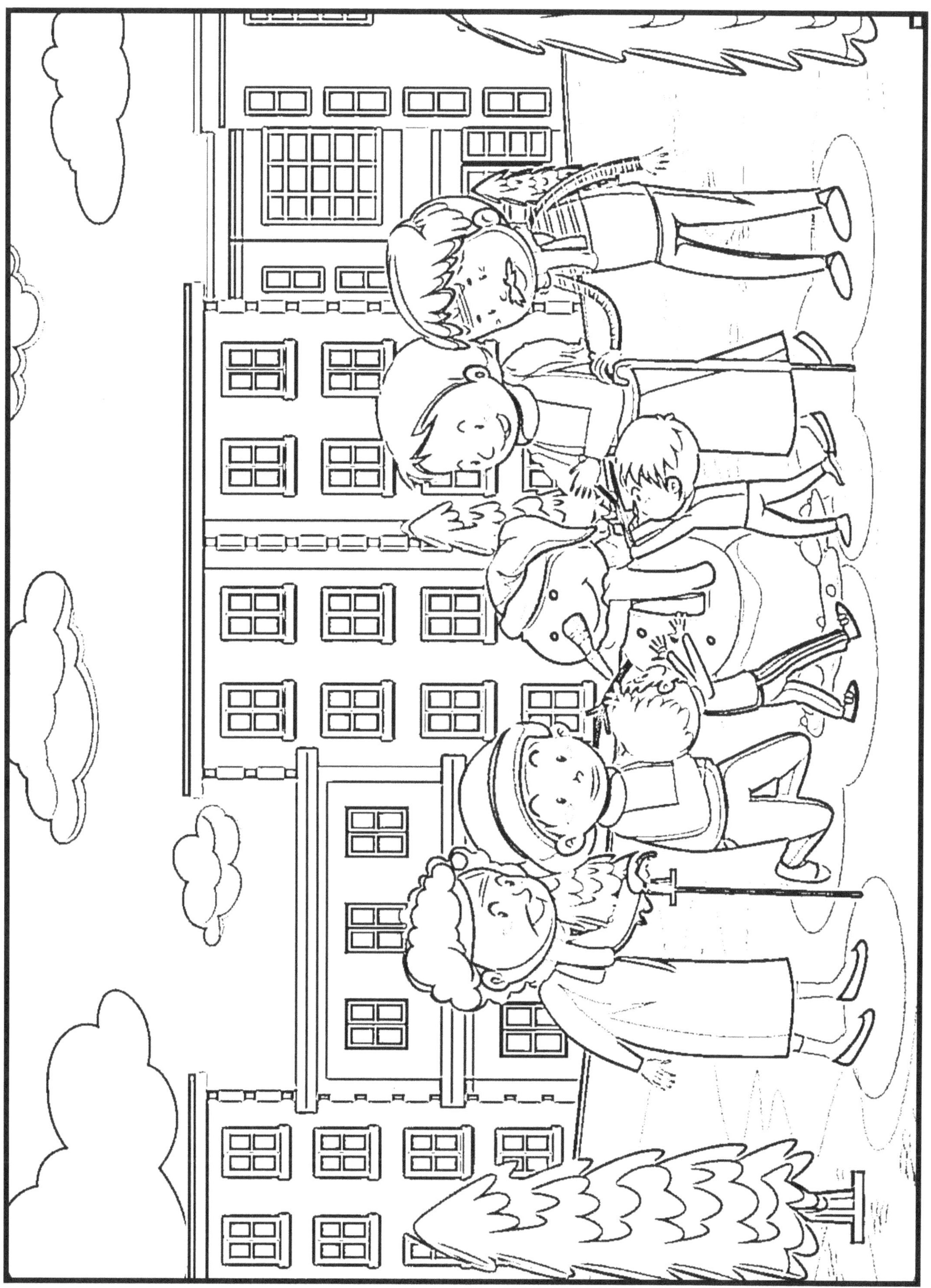

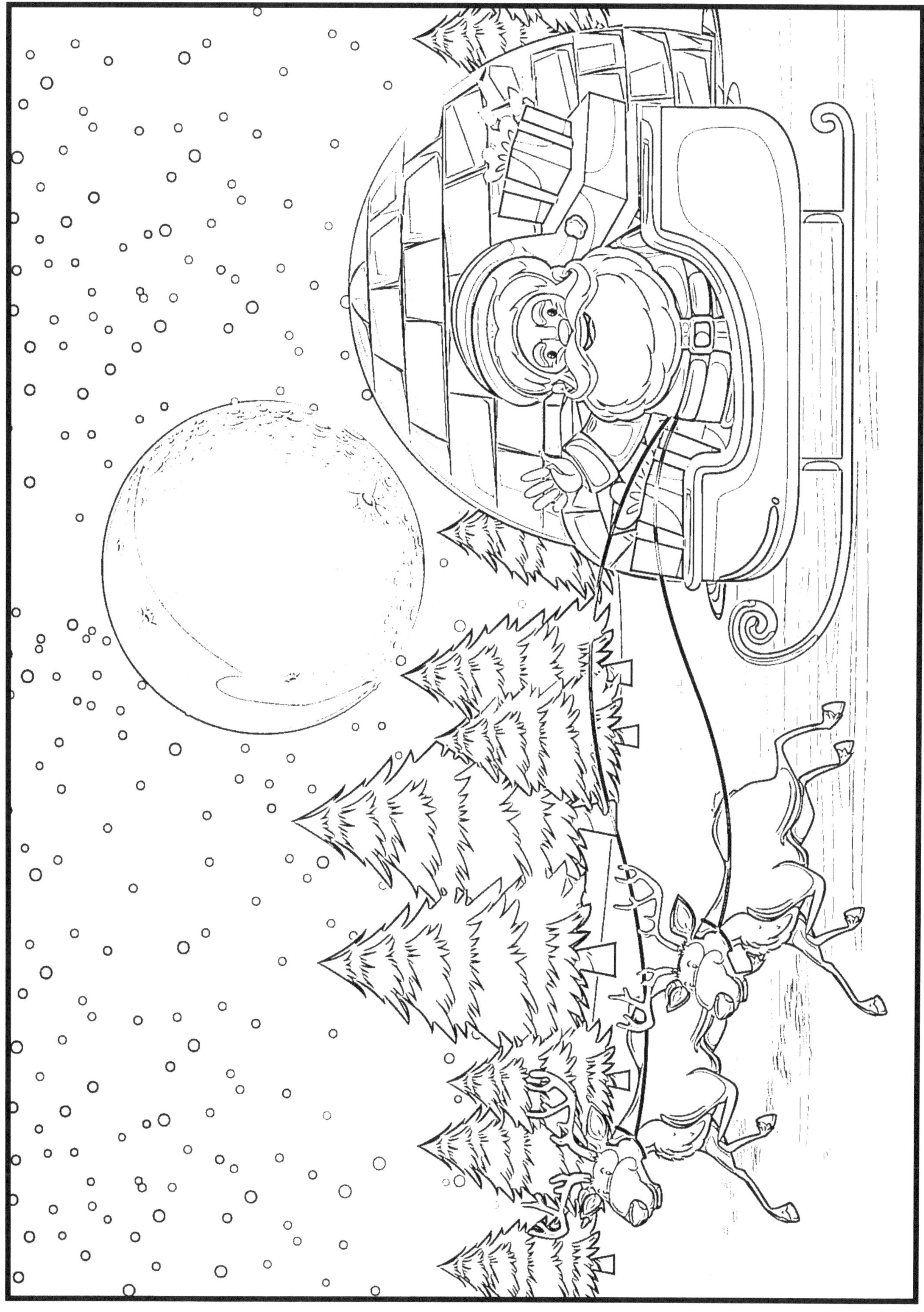

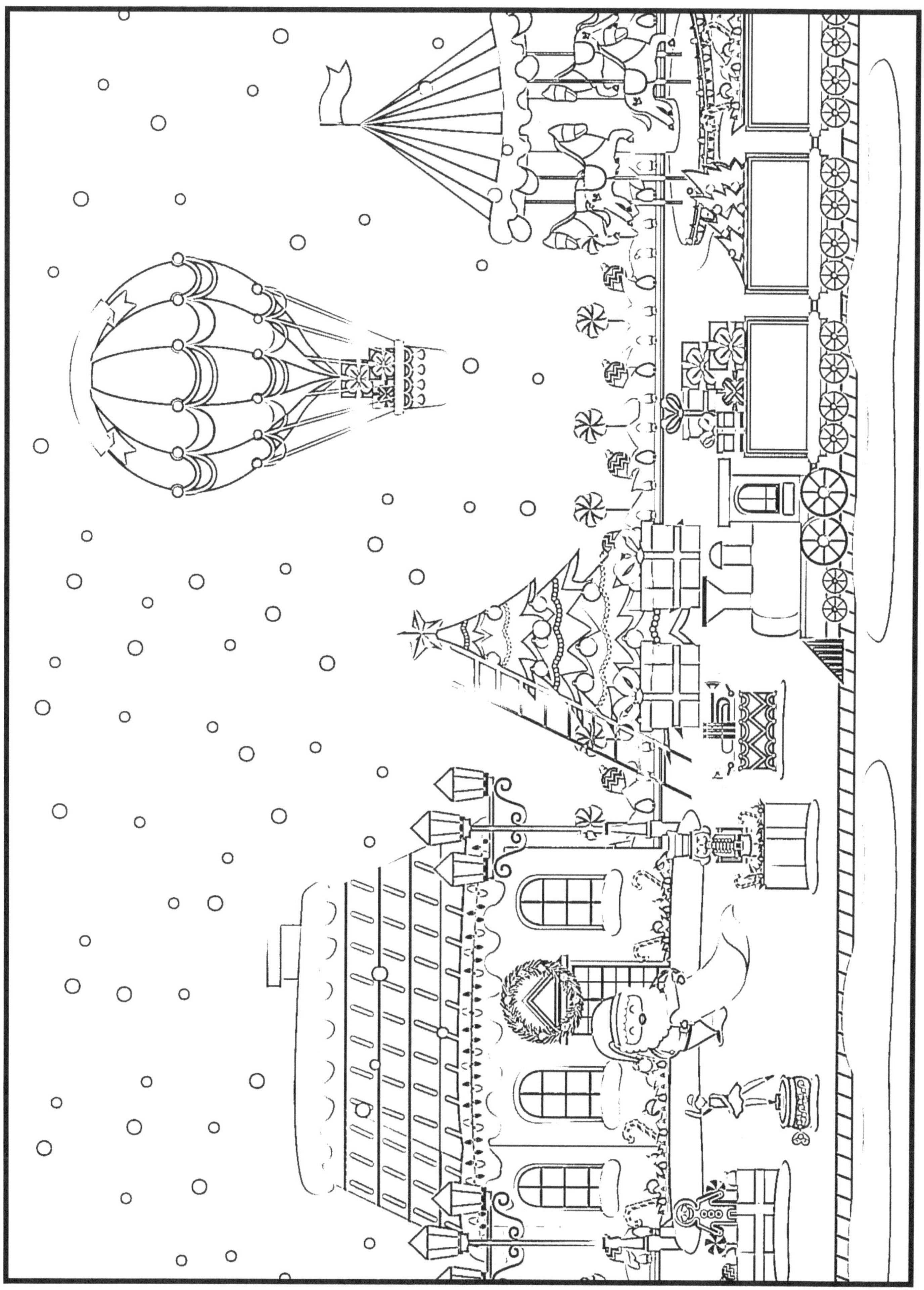

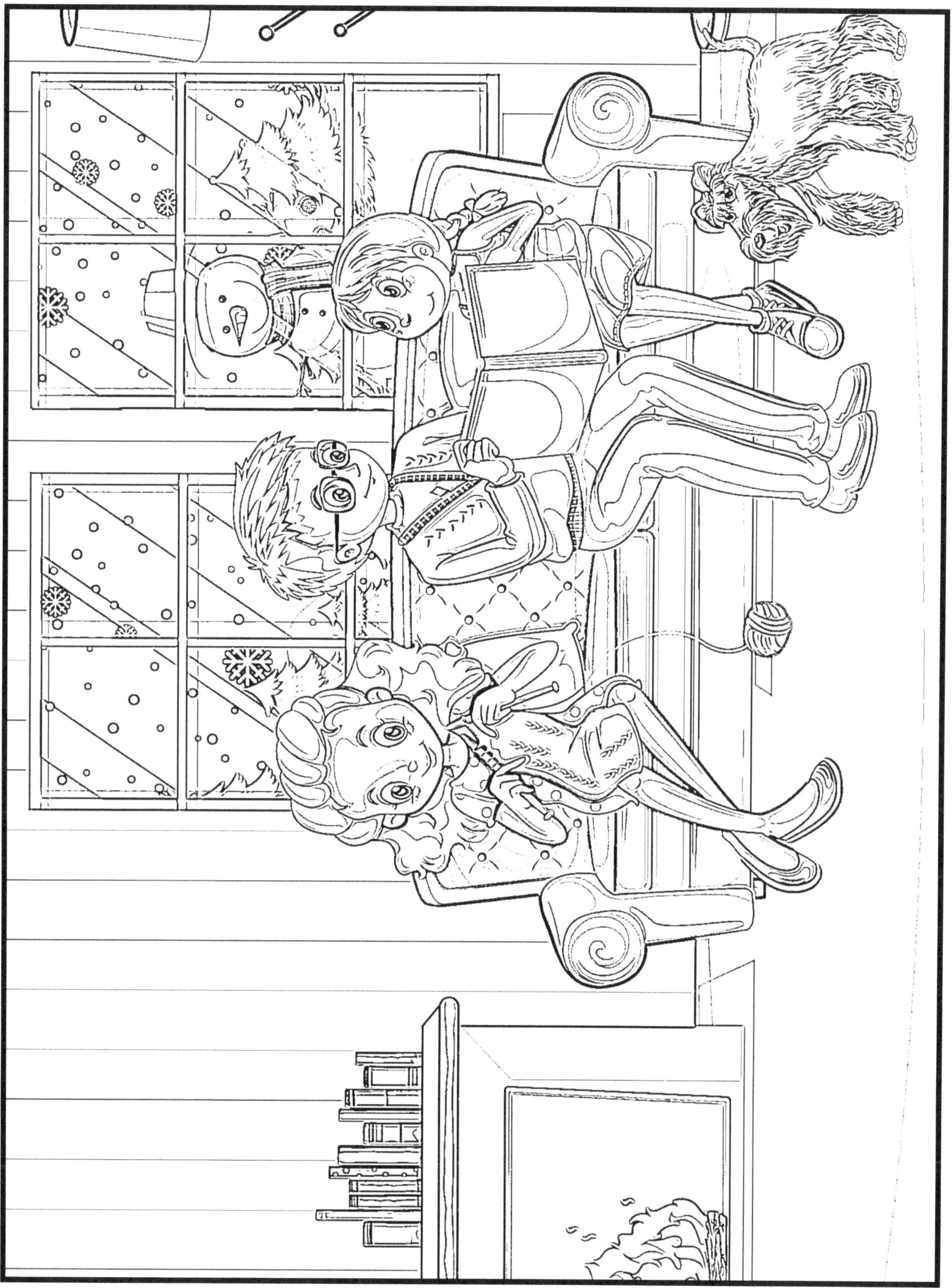

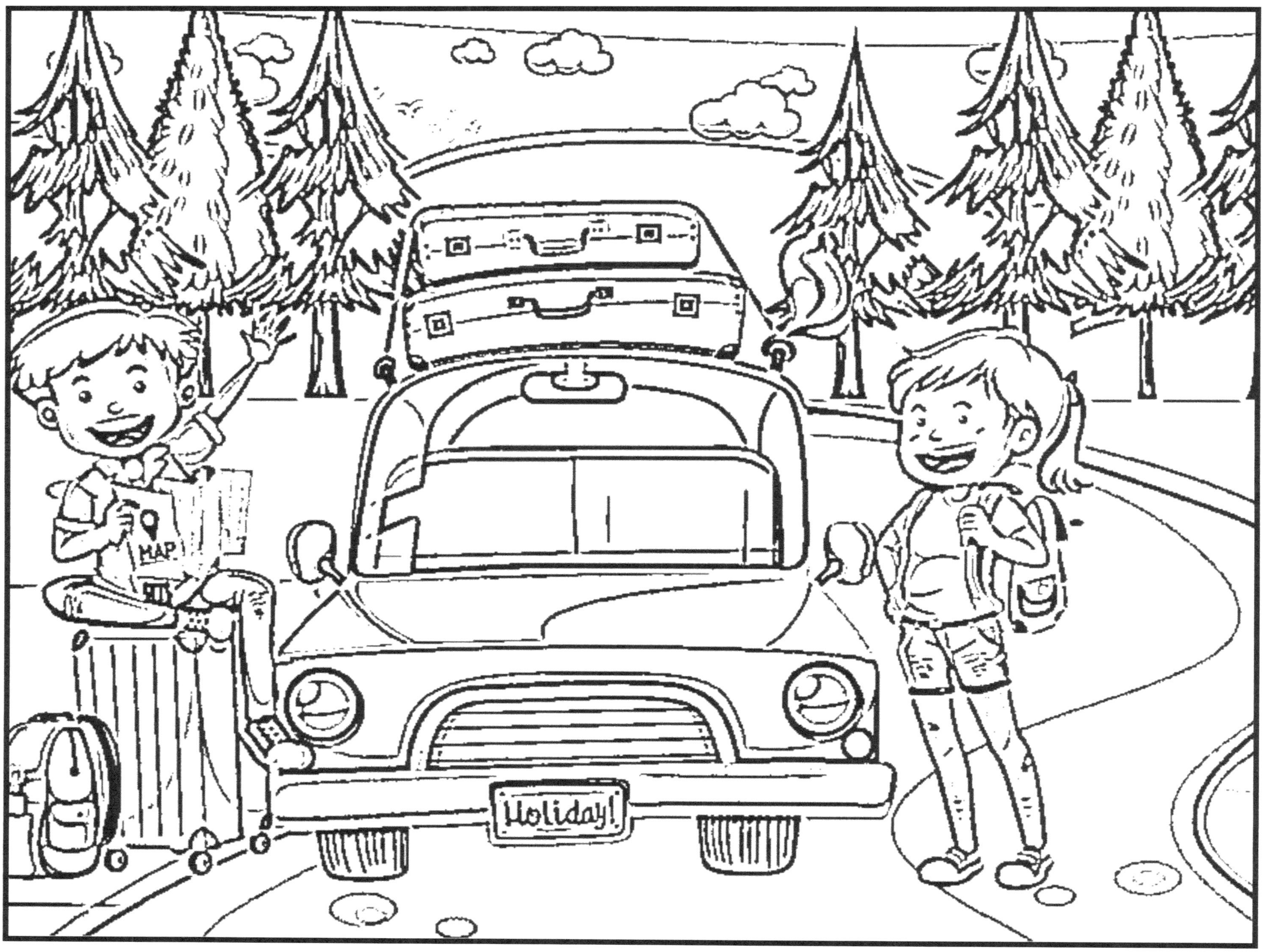

MAP
Holiday!

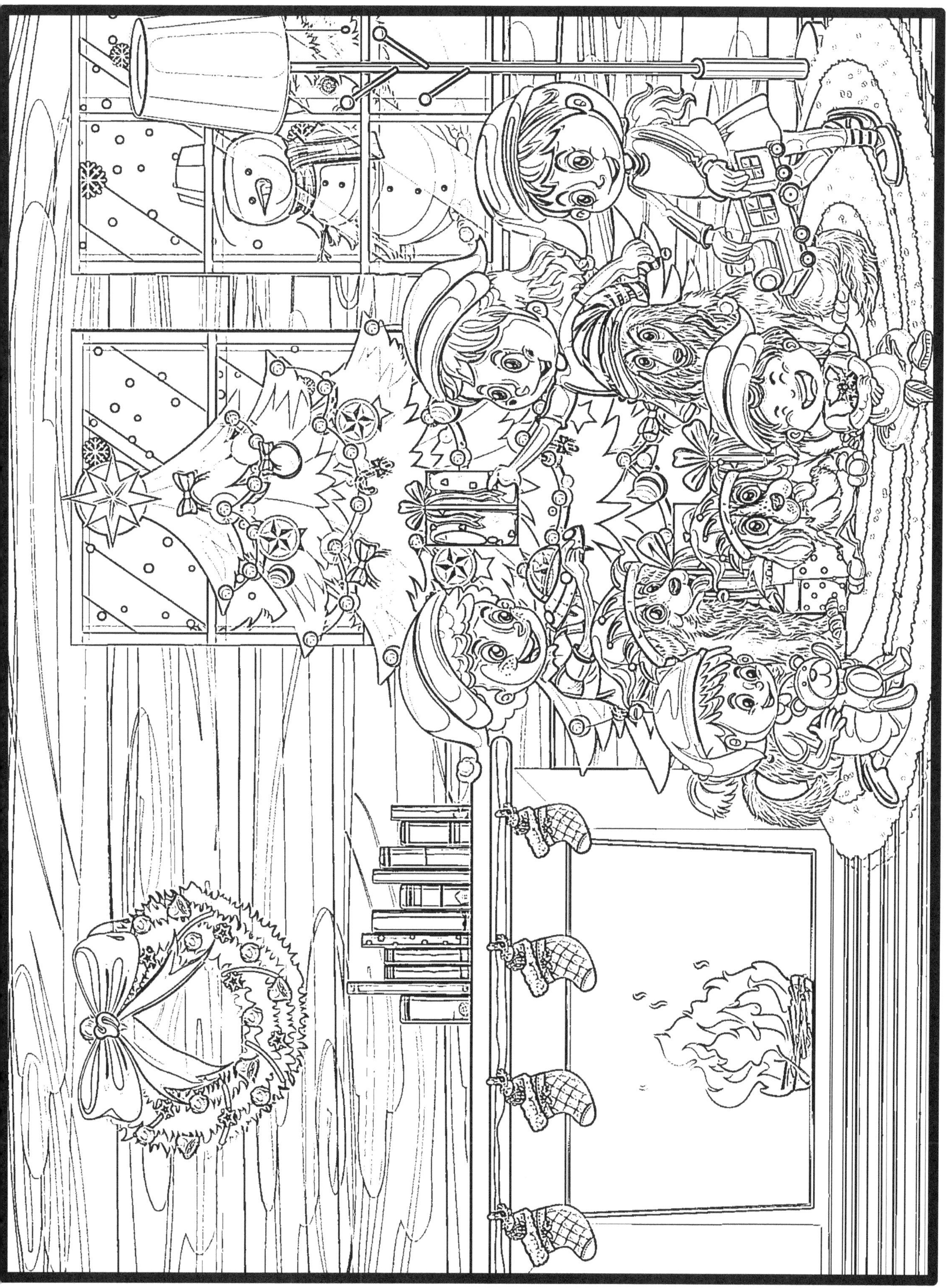

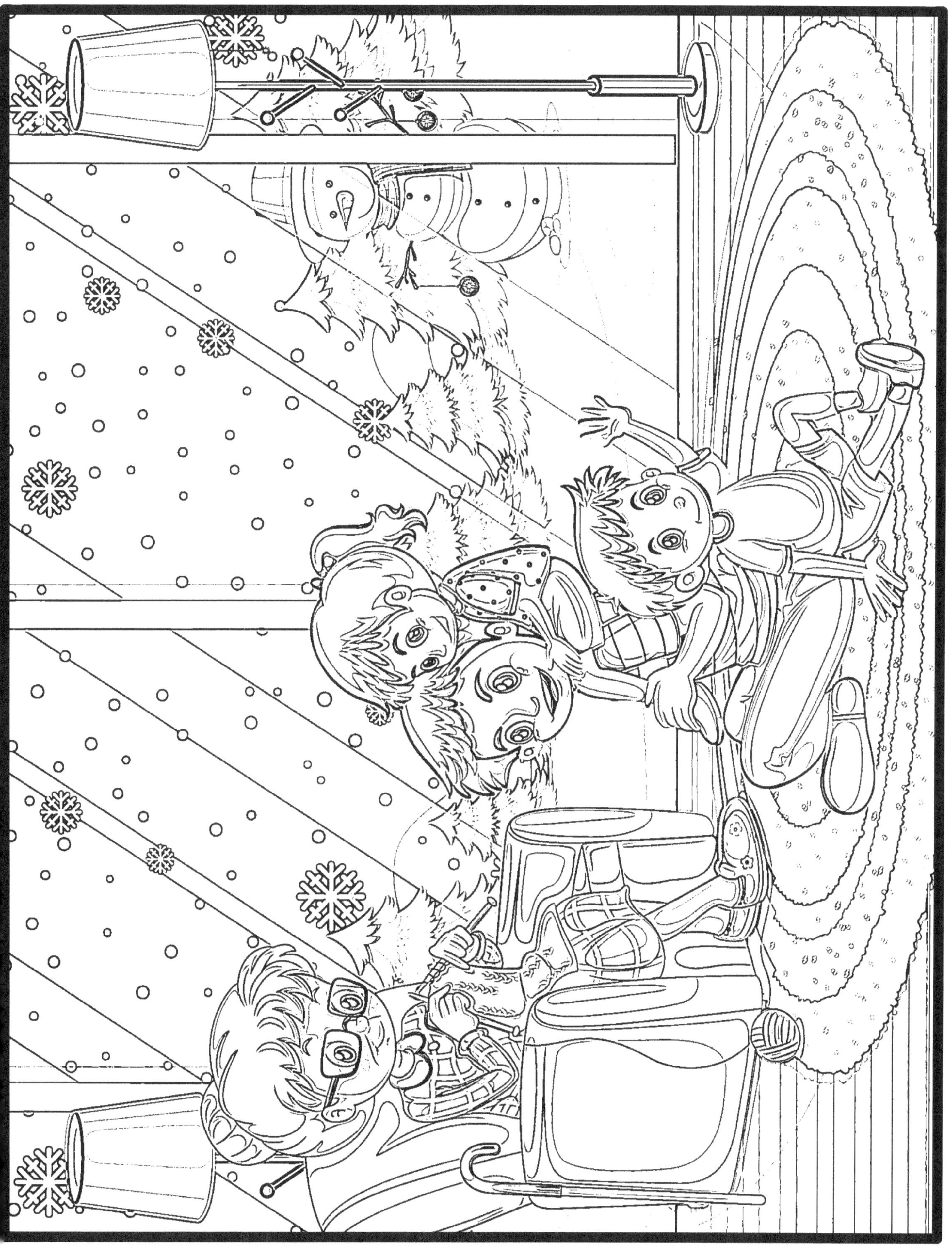

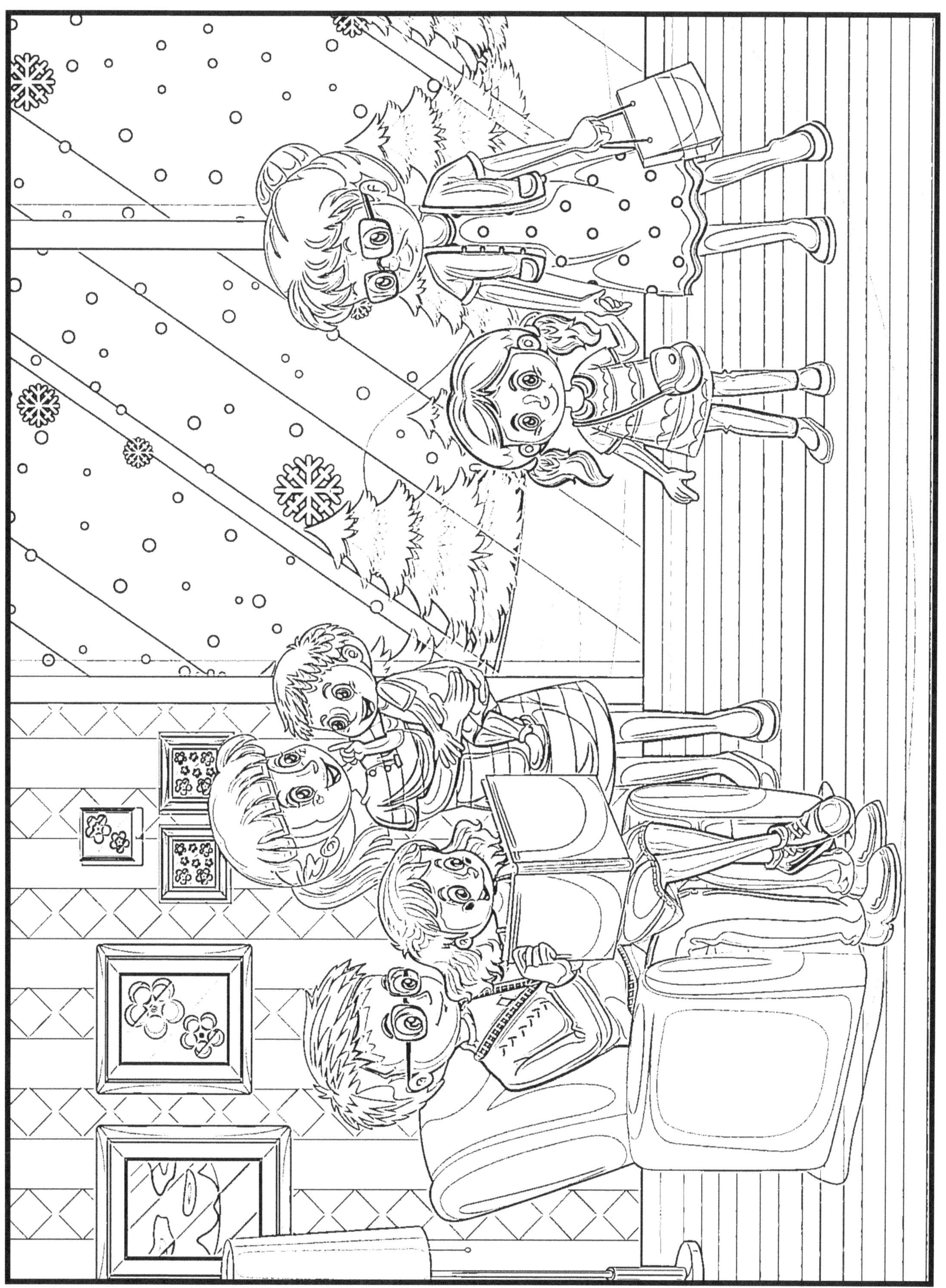

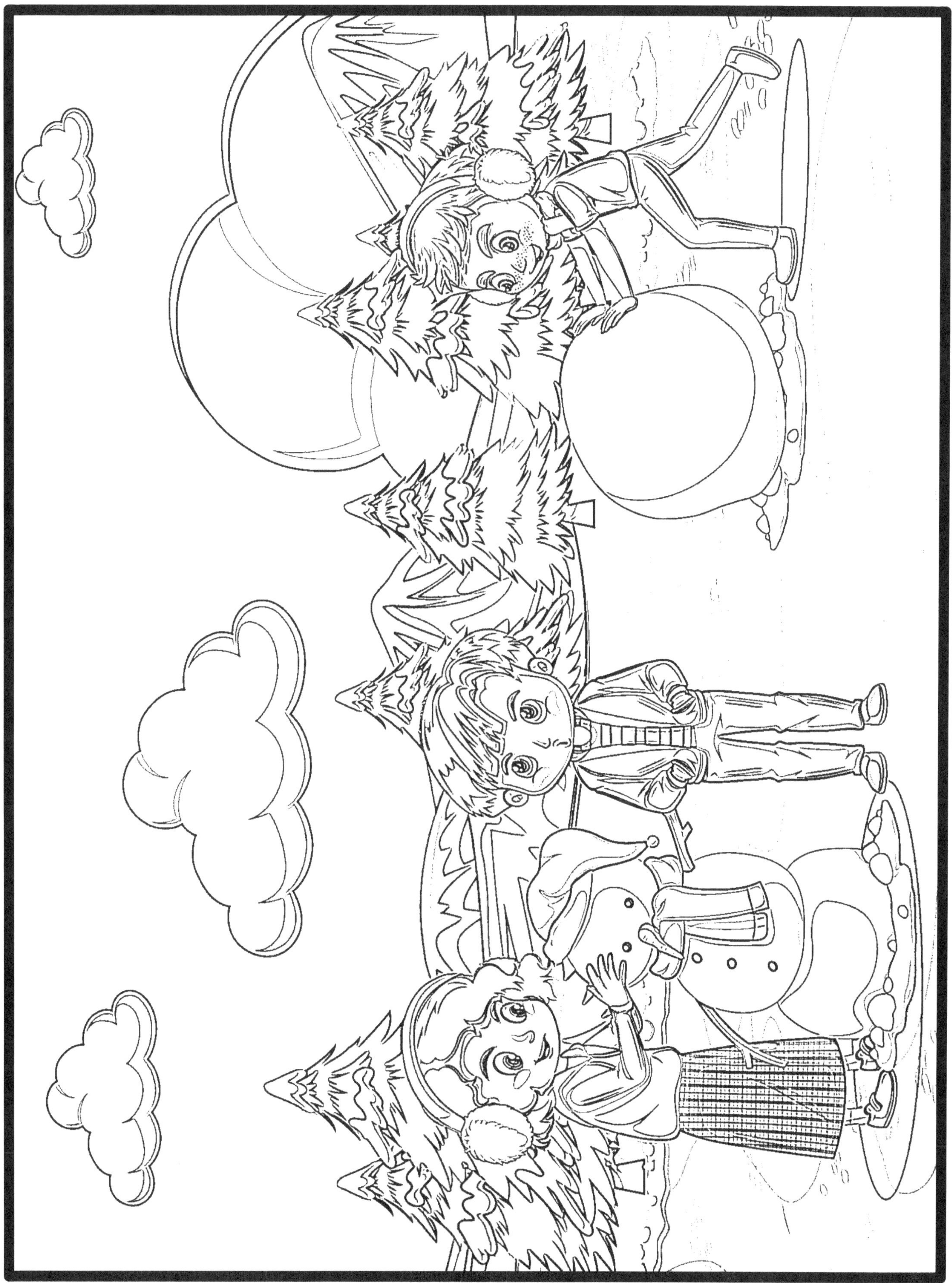

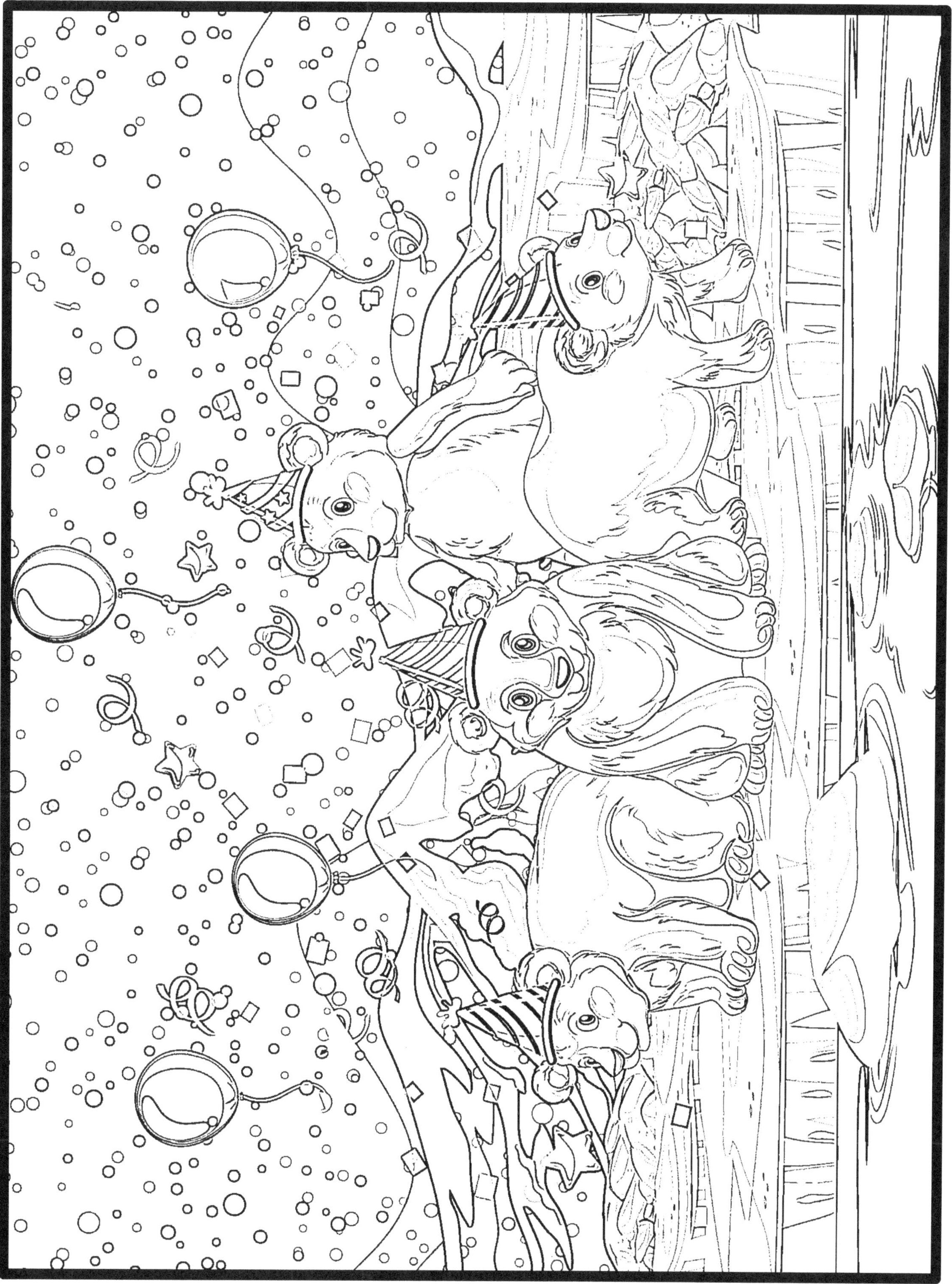

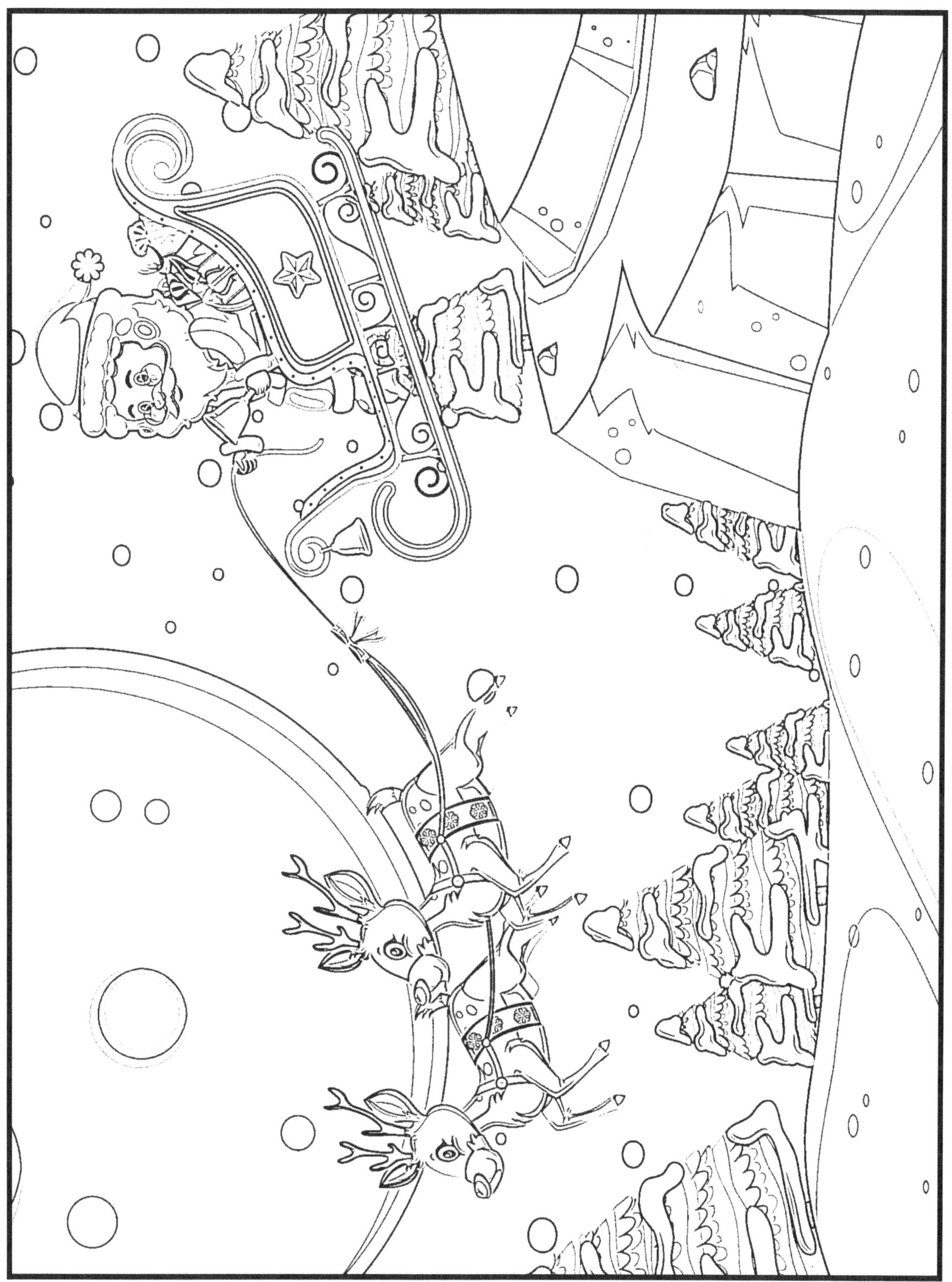

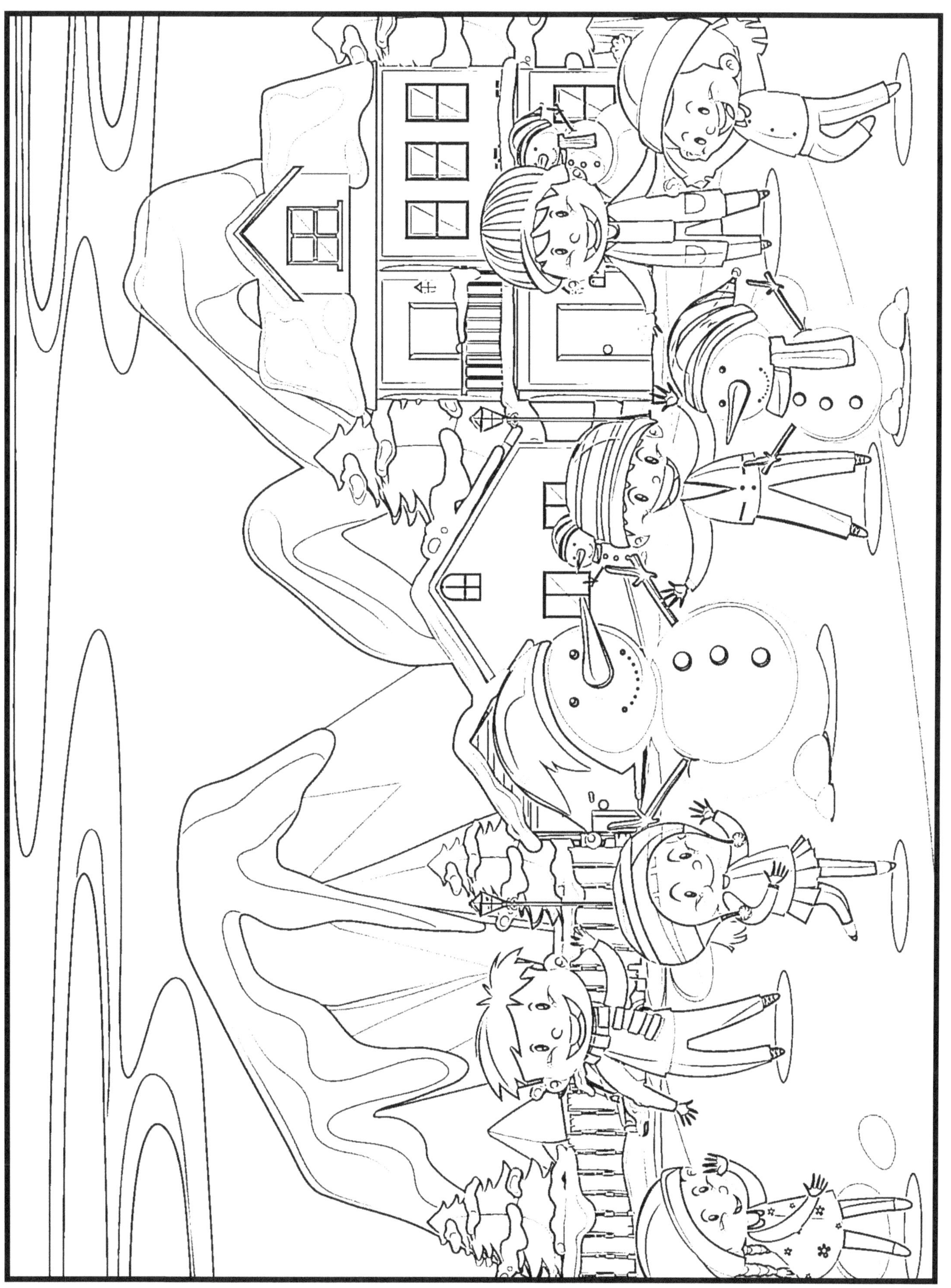